PRISON BREAK

A Couples Journey Into
Righteousness and Beyond the
Prison Walls

Nikkyea Williams

© 2014 by Nikkyea Williams.

All rights reserved. No part of this book may be reproduced, stored in a retrieval system or transmitted in any form or by any means without the prior written permission of the publishers, except by a reviewer who may quote brief passages in a review to be printed in a newspaper, magazine or journal.

First Printing

Revival Waves of Glory Books & Publishing has allowed this work to remain exactly as the author intended, verbatim, without editorial input.

Ebook 978-1-304-88560-9

Softcover 978-1-304-88558-6

Hardcover 978-1-304-88559-3

PUBLISHED BY REVIVAL WAVES OF GLORY
BOOKS & PUBLISHING
www.revivalwavesofgloryministries.com
Litchfield, IL

Printed in the United States of America

Table of Contents

INTRODUCTION 5

Chapter 1 THE BEGINNING MY DREAM 7

Chapter 2 THE CALL 13

Chapter 3 MY LITTLE SECRET 21

Chapter 4 DOING TIME 25

Chapter 5 VISITING TIME 31

Chapter 6 LEAD ME I'LL GO 37

Chapter 7 UNDERSTANDING 49

Chapter 8 LOOK TO THE SKY 53

Chapter 9 LISTEN AND OBEY 57

Chapter 10 G-O-E 61

Chapter 11 THE TRUTH SHALL SET YOU FREE 69

Chapter 12 RELEASED 75

Chapter 13 LETTING GO 81

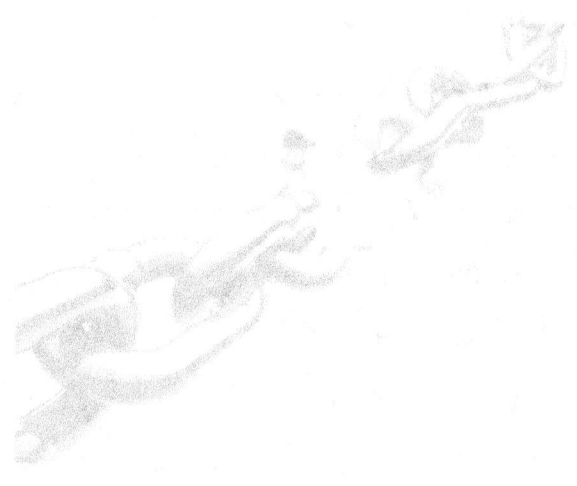

INTRODUCTION

Have you ever been broken?
I have, a few times.

I guess it depends on what kind of "break" you're speaking of.

I know that when you see the title "Prison Break" your mind instantly goes to a physical person breaking out of Prison…

That is just how the mind is programmed to think, but were going to change that thought pattern with this story.

This story is about a young woman who walked through a year and a half journey with a man that would be her mate…. Or not?

It will let you in on how she was broken in many different ways during this process and how God used her and built her into who she is today.

She had to be Broken in – in order to Break Forth and get Revelation and a Break-through

A couples Journey into righteousness and beyond the prison walls

Chapter 1

THE BEGINNING MY DREAM

"Great job ladies! You all ripped the runway! We will be posting the pictures and Videos on Social Media sites soon. I appreciate you all! Have a great night." Said Bianca. The owner of Sista Girl Boutique!

We had come to the end of the first full figured fashion show that I had participated in. Now all of the models, including myself, are leaving the show and heading to our separate destinations. The only difference is that everyone else is going home to someone, whether it's a Husband,

Fiancé, or boyfriend. But me, I was alone, well not technically. I've got my friend Ashley right by my side, who came out to support me, so she'll be hanging with me for the evening.

As we rode and talked about how wonderful the show was, I couldn't stop the thoughts that kept coming up in the back of my mind. I was thinking, why am I still single? What's really wrong with me? Other than, I refuse to settle for anything less than I deserve. Sigh. These thoughts kept getting stronger and louder, but I continued to engage in conversation about the show with Ashley.

When we made it back to my house I was so tired and my feet were overly sore from rocking those Fire Red Diba & Bronx heels all night. So I came in took a shower and headed for my Queen size Mattress. But first I had to talk to my daddy about a few things, there was no other way to end the night. So I got down on the side of my bed for some Knee Mail.

"Dear God, I come to you as humbly as I know how, thanking you for all you've done. God, why am I alone? I mean I know I am never alone with you but I mean a significant other.

I would really like a companion, someone to care about me, love and cherish me and my children. God is there a "real man" out there for me, a man after your own heart, or was I made to be alone? I only want your will to be done in my life. So God I am specifically asking you to send me a dream tonight and let me know if there is anyone out there just for me. Thank You Lord

In Jesus Mighty name I Pray.

AMEN."

I hopped up into my queen sized bed and drifted off to dreamland. Now I rarely have dreams, and when I do I really don't remember them, but I asked God for this dream. Then I went to bed with an expectancy of getting it and trusting and believing this dream would come to me tonight.

I slept oh so good that night. The next morning I woke up and rose with a stretch and a yawn and said, "Good morning Father! I thank you Lord for yet another day you have allowed me to see. I didn't have a dream last night but I still believe that you will give it to me and answer me in your timing! I Love you!"

I got up and headed for the bathroom, as I walked through the living room Ashley was sitting up on the couch having a morning cup of coffee! "Good Morning my Sista!" I say as I rush through to the bathroom. She responded, "Well Good morning."

A few minutes later I came back out of the bathroom and entered the living room. Ashley said "Oh hey Keisha, I had a dream about you last night." I paused, as my eyes bucked out! I gazed into the sky and then focused back in on her… "A dream about me?" I asked, as I pointed to myself. She answered "Yes." I took a very deep breath and I asked what it was about. "God has a man for you, he is just waiting on you to get yourself in order. I was sitting here, on the couch, in the dream and he was sitting across the table from me. He started to tell me that he loves you so much but you need to get yourself in order before he could be with you."

By this time my jaw was on the floor, I was so stunned in amazement. I was speechless for a moment, but when my words finally did inch out of my mouth I explained to Ashley that I had prayed for God to send me a dream about this situation. She said, "WOW, I had no idea!" I said,

"I know you didn't! God knows all and he is Simply Amazing."

Ashley proceeded to fill me in on the dream. She told me that the man in the dream was not the type of man that I would usually talk to at all. She went on to say, "I remember his head being big, not in a sense that he has a big head but just that he is a real man. Head of the home type, one who takes care of his family and responsibilities. He is a real man, a family man, a man of God. He is a bit older than you, his skin is a shade lighter than mine (light skin complexion).

He is a tad bit taller than me, maybe about 5'10"······ Oh forget all that, you've just got to see him! Yea, you've just got to see him that's all. Then you will know what I am talking about." I was puzzled and a bit anxious, but I said "ok."

I pondered on this conversation that me and Ashley had for about 3 days. I mean God is so amazing! I asked him specifically to give me a dream, and he sent my dream to me through my friend who was spending the night at my house. Then made sure she delivered it to me the next morning. Ashley had dreams and visions about her friends sometimes, but she did not always share them. This much I did know about her.

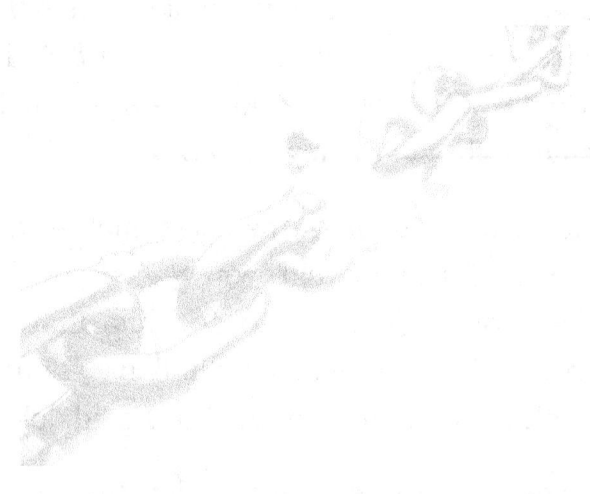

Chapter 2

THE CALL

Now that I had received some instruction on what to do, I began to work on some things. I started to get myself in order because I knew that when I did, things would start happening as they should.

I started to cook more, clean more, stock up on household things, got my children in order, and interacted with them more, attending church more often and missing church far less. I felt as if I was changing for the better, getting a bit of order you know? Work, Home, Church, yep that was pretty much my life.

When I went to work, God would use me to speak to different people while on the job, saying things that he wanted me to say and giving those scriptures to read. Though it was risky because I could have lost my job doing it, I had to obey God. As I did this God kept me covered as I spoke what he wanted me to say. Ministry is what it was called. I did it just about every single day that I worked at this place so it was a normal part of my daily schedule, even though sometimes I did not want to say things to people.

One day as I sat at my desk and prepared to take my break, my cell phone rang. When I picked up and looked at the phone the call came from an 877 number. I knew this number looked familiar but I wasn't sure what I would hear on the other end of the phone when I said hello······

So I went for it, "Hello" I said. Instantly a recording came on saying··· This is a Prepaid Collect call from "It's me" at Benson Correctional Center, to accept this call press #1.

My mind started to move a mile a minute wondering, who, what, hoping that this isn't one of my family members or close friends calling me to say they had gotten themselves locked up. So I braced myself and pressed the #1. "Hello" I said. Then the voice on the other end of the phone said my name, "Keisha!" I paused and said, "Yea, who is this?" He proceeded, "This is

Mikey" I scratched my head with a puzzled mindset. I know this couldn't be the Mikey I think it is. I just simply took a deep breath and hung the phone up on him. Click.

2 min went by and my phone started to ring again from that same number, I clicked reject as I went off like why is my ex-boyfriend calling me from prison? How did he even get my phone number, where did he come from, it's been 3 years, didn't he get married? Leave me alone, shoot!

After pressing reject 4 more times the phone continued to ring. He was not giving up. So I answered the phone again, Pressed #1 and said "WHAT!!! Who is this? Is this a Joke? You're kidding me right?" He responded "This is Mikey, and naw I'm not playing, do I sound like I'm playing? I wouldn't be calling you if I was playing!" I paused again. "Is this Mikey Smithson?" "No this is Mikey Mason." Now I was very confused because I knew I did't know this person.

"So how do you know me Mikey and how did you get my number? Because Uhmmmm I don't know you." He said "You don't remember me? I met you a year ago online."

I went on listening to this foolishness because that's exactly what it was to me. I hadn't met or given anyone my new number since it's been changed for 5 months now, but I listened and let him dig his hole deeper. Because this dude was obviously lying.

I stated, "I don't know you Mikey, and I didn't give you my number so who did?" I had not been on a Social Media sight in so long, though I tried it, it just wasn't for me.

He continued on "You do know me, you gave me your number a year ago and we talked very briefly. I'm calling now because I will be home soon, and I'm just looking for a friend."

I continued to stand on what I knew, and I knew that I did not know this man. "Sir I don't know you at all." He then replied. "Keisha you know me, you just have to see me."

I took a deep breath, my heart skipped a beat at that very moment. "What did you just say?" I asked. He repeated himself, "I said you just have to see me that's all."

Those words started it all, it took me back to the dream I had prayed for and then me and Ashley's conversation. All I could hear was

Ashley in my ear saying···. "You just have to see him, It's not anyone that you would normally go for, and when you least expect it he will find you. Just stay focused on God and getting yourself together. He will come."

But really? This has got to be a mistake! I'm not going to even think this would ever be the way to get my attention. Ugh. Those words were the only reason our conversation went any further.

I stopped and took a deep breath and said, "Well let me hear what you have to say because this could very well be an assignment from God."

"Really!" He replied. "I can talk to you about God too! That's what's up! So do you go to church Keisha? If so what church do you go to? We have services up here and I go every Sunday.

I stated that I attended Change Christian Church and I loved my church home and the Lord. And as much as I would've liked to listen and get some more understanding of what was going on, my break at work was coming to an end. So I said "excuse me Mikey this was a nice convo but my break is just about up so I have to get back to work now".

"Ok, look Keisha I don't want anything from you, all I need is a friend to talk to from time to time, maybe write and things of that sort. Now that I know that you are a Woman of God, I can really talk to you. Would you mind if I called you sometimes just to chat when I am able? Then if we decided to write or whatever else later on that would all be up to you"... I paused for a good 30 seconds wondering if I really wanted to open up this door by saying yes. Then I said it, "sure that should be fine."

"Ok. Keisha, God Bless you goodbye."

Now things were slow motion at work and I was in deep doubt as I gazed at the ceiling and said "really God? This can't be, I know you wouldn't send me anyone incarcerated this has got to be a test! Who is this man? How did he find me? Prison? This is crazy what could I ever get out of or learn from this."

As I sat there in a lawless state, I heard my spirit say to me "you prayed for patience, how badly you want it?" All I could do was slump down in my chair. As I sat there God dropped (James 2) in my spirit. I opened up my New Living Translation Bible to see the headline "A warning against prejudice" as I read the passage I just wanted to scream! What is happening! I couldn't do anything else but smile and say, Thank you God, I trust you! Just as I finished reading the scripture my work phone rang and back to the workflow I went.

Chapter 3

MY LITTLE SECRET

A week had gone by and I hadn't mumbled a word about my mysterious phone call to a single soul. I mean seriously, why would I? That was nothing I was going to shout out on the rooftop. I wasn't even going to whisper it I just kept it between God and me.

Exactly 7 days later I got that call again. Just like last time the conversation was good. In jail, out of jail, even in my face, it's hard for a man to keep my attention with conversation so this good conversation was a plus.

We talked about the Scriptures and God, but I had other things in mind I wanted answered. "Look, our conversation is on point, you and me both love and are continuing our conversation about God right?

Well, God is love and God is the truth and you started this friendship off wrong by lying. I know for a fact that I did not give you my number so how did you get it?" He then replied, "Okay look I called a friend of mine and I told him I was lonely and needed someone to talk to, he went through his phone and gave me your number."

Wow! Now that's crazy, we really have to be careful who we issue our information out to. We talked for maybe five minutes more then he expressed that he would reach back out when he put some more minutes on his phone card. I said, "Okay talk to you later, God Bless"

I really wanted to share this info about these phone calls with someone. But I knew that was not an option that I had at that moment so I just continued to hold it in.

Five days had passed and the third phone call was made. "Hey hey how are you my sister?" I replied, "Hello there, I'm blessed." We then started to converse. In mid conversation he started to ask me about my church history. I told him that I had grown up at my family church on the North side of St. Louis Mo. The name of the church is Congregational COGIC Church where Pastor Nathan Clark is my uncle. "What! Pastor Clark is your family?"

"Yes" I replied. "Wow that's the first church I ever went to, your uncle was cool. I attended church there with my aunt Leslie and my cousin Davion. The church van use to pick us up on Sundays."

"Really!" I replied, "well my dad drove the church van for as far back as I can remember."

So the more we talked the more people we found out we had in common. I knew his aunt and cousin very well, and he grew up around my God family. He even expressed that he was a very good boxer and he was taught by the best, my very own Godfather, a boxing Guru that is. Now I was feeling a bit more comfortable. We have all these people in common, the conversation is great and interesting, but Prison is the problem! But who am I to judge? Most have taken Penitentiary chances. Some of us were just blessed not to go.

He goes on to ask me if it would be alright for him to get my address so he could write me a short letter and send me a picture of himself. Again I paused. Now mind you that at this point in the game of course I've done my research on this guy. I found out how many times he had been to prison, why he went, made sure he was not a murderer, a pedophile, etc. I'm not judging just had to make sure, it only made sense. But after a bit of consideration I answered "Sure what could be the harm in that?" Plus I was looking forward to seeing who this mystery man was. After all, remember, I just had to see him.

As I provided him with the information so he could write me, I continued to think in the back of my mind···. Really Lord, Prison? Sigh. I asked for patience but not this way. I asked for a man, but I'd much rather him be free and able to take care of and provide for me. I can't see that happening with a man incarcerated. I couldn't see one thing that an incarcerated man could do for me a "free as a bird woman". I had no idea what the future had in store for me.

Chapter 4

DOING TIME

About two days had passed and I received a letter from Distant Correctional Center. This was it! I opened the letter to see a very short letter and a picture. The man on the picture was very handsome and nearly a splitting image of the man Ashley described in the dream, from age to his height and skin tone. I was outdone. I decided I couldn't hold it in any longer I had to share what I've been holding in for a while now. Well at least with Ashley, because I didn't know how people would take this man being jail. So I got on the phone and I called up my girl and asked her to come over. Ashley did not live far from me so she was at my doorstep within 10 minutes.

When Ashley got to my house I was a bit hesitant, but I say it "girl okay, I have a taxicab confession." A taxicab confession equals juicy gossip, so Ashley was immediately tuned in. I started by taking her back to the night she had the dream, and then I told her that I met a man. Ashley's jaw dropped in excitement as she exclaimed really! "Yep", I replied. I explained that He called me out of the blue and we had been talking ever since. I told her that he was a little bit taller, a little bit lighter, a tad bit older, and most definitely not the type of man I would usually go for... PERIOD. Again Ashley said, "Really"? "Yes Ma'am, I can show you a picture if you'd like." I said

"Oh wow! You have a picture? Sure girl let me see!" So I pulled out my picture that I had of him and handed it to her as I took a deep breath and said" He's incarcerated when he said to me, you just need to see me, then I immediately went back to the dream that I prayed for/ that you had." "WOW" she said as her eyes got big and her jaw dropped to the floor. "He is very nice looking and his description is on point with what I said and what I saw in my dream, but all I am going to say to you is to stay in the spirit on this one. You never know when a person is in Prison. There are some that are real when it comes to going all out for God on the inside, but then again there are some imposters that just have that time on their hands. Again just stay before God and remain friends with this guy and you will be ok." I knew I would be able to count on Ashley for some straight forward non-judgmental advice on something like this here. And I totally appreciated her for that.

Later on that evening Mikey called. "Hello my sister how are you?" "Hey Mikey Mike I'm good and you? I got your picture and yes you are a nice looking man." Thanks, he replied. We went on with our conversation just as usual. He explained to me that he just left his parole hearing he had been waiting on and that had went before the board and they had given him a date to come home! I was extra excited to hear this news. "When do you come home?" I asked in excitement. He replied "September 2013." Silence hit the airways for about 2 minutes straight. I mean it was April 2012 right now.

Mikey broke the silence by saying "I know that is a long time from now, and if you do not want to continue on talking to me then I understand. But I am excited and thankful to God because I was supposed to do much more time than that, so I will take it. Thank God!" I was still soaking this in, I mean we are friends, nothing more so I spoke out. "Ok my friend, I will be around, we are still friends!" He gave a sigh of relief as he told me that he would be changing facilities soon and would be getting released for work daily. We then made a pact that if we continued to speak to each other for 3 more months, then on that 4th month, I would come up to visit him.

About a month and a half had passed and Mikey was transferred to the Edgemont Facility of Corrections. We continued to talk and write. God was the center of everything we spoke on and did, we prayed, had bible study, he tested me on the Word of God to the point I was thinking Wow! Here I am talking about this being an assignment for me and this man knows more than I do, he is helping my growth process tremendously when it comes down to getting into the word. There were times where I felt like I was the assignment for him. Mikey would listen to me talk about my problems and give me good advice. Mainly because he always went to the Word of God! He would always take me to Ephesians 6 and say read this and recite it every day Keisha! Put on the Whole armor of God!

Then he loved to hit on Galatians 5, the fruits of the spirit! If I was mad or down or whatever he always had a word to pick me up. Even if he was the reason I was mad, because we had a few disagreements by this time. But the biggest and best thing he would say to me and keep on reminding me was "Stay in the Word Keisha!"

But as well as he helped me I was being a help to him also. We were each other's helpmates! I was praying like never before and I prayed for him all the time. I started to hear and recognize the voice of God even more than I did before.

After 2 weeks at the new Facility, Mikey called me and he sounded down, he was telling me that his caseworker was dragging her feet on getting him out to work, and he was so ready to get outside of those 4 walls.

That night I got on my knees got Jesus on the Mainline and started to speak to that situation with authority, I declared and decreed that the caseworker would not procrastinate his case another second, that she would get this man of God out to work immediately In Jesus mighty name, Amen.

I did not hear from Mikey until 3 days later, He was calling to inform me that the day after we talked his caseworker approved his work release and he was out working 2 days later. Praise God, Prayer works! Mikey said "I know you were praying Keisha! I thank God for you daily because you truly are my Angel! I prayed and asked God to send me a friend, but I never ever imagined it would be like this! I am ready to see you Keish! I need to hug you in my arms!" Mikey went on to remind me that we were approaching 4 months and asked how I felt about coming to visit him. I was ok with it so in 3 more weeks I'd be going to visit Mikey in person for the first time.

Chapter 5

VISITING TIME

That 3 weeks flew past and it was time for me to keep my promise and head out to see Mikey. He was about 2 ½ hours from where I lived so it was a long peaceful ride. When I approached the facility, I immediately got a little shaky. I am about to be locked in for hours, I don't do well with being confined period. I park my car, get out and go through the front doors to be buzzed into the next door where there's a guard asking for my ID. Then I'm asked to take off my jewelry and empty my pockets. Next I go through the metal detectors and to a window to sign in, then to the next guard who does the drug scope to make sure I was not bringing drugs inside. Once cleared there, my hand was stamped and I was buzzed through 2 more doors and into the visiting room where I had to meet yet another guard to get a table number.... After all of that I was on edge and super shook up. My goodness! After waiting a good 30 minutes Mikey entered the room. He came up to me and gave me an extra tight hug and then from there we instantly started to connect face to face.

We talked, read the word, talked about the word, played a few games and enjoyed each other's company down until the last minute when I had to get up and leave. At that time all that I had to go through to get into that visiting room was forgotten because it was so worth it.

After that milestone in our friendship we talked even more than we did before. I believe we both felt even more connected like we had known each other forever. Shortly thereafter I had a phone account set up to where I would put minutes on every now and then so that we could talk a little more than we already did. There were a few times when I was led to be a blessing and put a few dollars on his books, then there were other times when I just did it on my own.

Mikey and I talked more, we wrote each other more, and we got to know each other more. We had a spiritual connection. I started to feel him in my spirit to where I could finish his sentences, or know what was going on without even being around him, so I would just pray for him. It was a bit scary but it was a good feeling to have a friend like that, that I had gained trust for. We would just "Keep it Real" with each other. He had become my best friend. We may become more once he is home but for now we were just friends.

There were a few times I would call some of Mikey's family and friends on the 3 way. I remember a family member got on the phone and started to converse with him and the word "trust" fell in my spirit. I shared this with Mikey after we got off the 3 way call. He called me back the next day and said "Hey Keisha, you are truly my Angel from God. He told me why I had heard the word trust. He had just talked to a friend of his that informed him that the same family member he was conversing with had been running around telling lies on him. I could not say anything but "WOW".

Now at this point Mikey and I were still friends, he had told a few people about me, including his mother, but as for me, my lips were still sealed. I saw no reason to inform people of this friendship. Mikey really was not happy about this because he felt I should tell people about our friendship/relationship. He expressed to me that he felt I was embarrassed by it, because it was now a year later and it's still my little secret. I explained to him that if I am going to talk and tell people about you then I would rather you be my man and a free man at that. Free to come visit and meet people. Not in prison. I did not feel that me speaking on this was a big deal at this point. But I did believe that this story we would have to tell in the end would be an awesome testimony. But I had not said a mumbling word about it to anyone except for Ashley.

I loved Mikey at this point. I mean that's what we were telling each other now. I Love You! Agape-Love that is Unconditional Love. I mean I talked to this man more than I talked to anyone else, he knew all about me and what was going on in my life, he was my best friend my confidant, an all-around good person who made a wrong decision that landed him where he was, in prison.

In this last year of my life, I have consulted God and stayed in his face more than ever before. I expected more, my faith level has elevated. I have seen God moving on me and my family's behalf more. My relationship with God has gotten more intimate because I spend more time with God and my desire was to be closer to him and for God to remain at the center of this relationship. Because now I am getting letters that say, "Keisha you've been there for me, I can't believe you're still around and you hold me down like you do. You pray for and with me, I really owe you me. I can't see it any other way than me making you my wife. I Love you & I owe you a ring!" My instant reply was "You don't owe me anything, the things I do I do out of Love. Nothing more nothing less. So if you want to thank anyone thank God, not me. "I was starting to think, does this man really love me or does he love the things that I do for him⋯.

Chapter 6

LEAD ME I'LL GO

One weekend I made up in my mind to take a weekend trip down to where Mikey was so that I could visit with him 2 days in a row on Saturday and Sunday. My mindset was to visit Saturday get up and go to church on Sunday morning and then go visit him on Sunday afternoon after service.

When I got into the visiting room on Saturday, I went over to pick up the Bible, a deck of cards and a connect 4 game. I loved to play connect 4 even though Mikey couldn't stand it. He said it was a kiddie game, but he still played it with me and we had so much fun. I always whooped his tail in it. But our visit went awesome as expected. We played the games and read and talked about the word. One thing Mikey was adamant about was word. I must admit we talked about that word and God more than anything else. He knew his word and he made sure I stayed in mine. It was like I was in some kind of training. He would ask me questions and if I didn't know the answer or where to find it in the word, he would give me a sermon.

This time as he was preaching the guard told everyone that visit time was ending. So we said our goodbye's and I headed back to the next small town to sit down and have a meal before I decided what hotel I was going to stay in for the night. I came across a magazine stand that held free coupon books so I picked one up and it had just the deal I needed for a room. I said "Thank You God" as I headed to the hotel. I got to the hotel and checked into my room, that I paid a little bit of nothing for with my coupon. I walked into a living room then on through to the bedroom. It was like a one-bedroom shotgun apartment.

Now that I was here, I took my shower and laid across the bed to relax. As I got comfortable my phone rang. It was Mikey calling to make sure all was well and I had found a place. I assured him that I did, immediately he said "man I love you, and I am so grateful to God for you Keisha! I really do love you, you hear me?" I said "yes, I love you too." Then he asked me "what time are you coming up here tomorrow?" "Well, I was thinking about going to church in the morning, but I think I'm going to just come see you in the morning and go home before it gets too late." I said. He replied, "No, you need to get up and go on to church in the morning, go on and give God the praise then you can come and we can talk about it, at least you can go to church. They cut out our services and here so we don't get to have service. You go ahead and get some rest sweetie so you can get up and go to church, I'm going to call you in the morning okay?" "Alright." I replied

I got curled up in the bed and dozed off to sleep. My alarm clock went off at 8:30 a.m. I hopped up to start preparing myself for church when all of a sudden; God dropped something in my spirit along with a scripture for me to give to one of my closest friends. I started to wonder if I was just tripping or if this was something I needed to do, it didn't take long for me to figure it out. I wasn't going to fight it I just picked up my phone and sent a text message to my friend wondering how this would play out, because this was new to me. But what did I do not know at the moment, is that it was a test of my faith/obedience to prepare me for what else was going to happen very soon. I had to be obedient to God.

Just then my friend text back and said thank you I received that word. Then I exhaled, thank you God!

As I continue getting myself ready Mikey (my other daddy) call to make sure I was getting ready for church as well as letting me know he was looking forward to our visit this afternoon. The feeling was mutual, I could not wait to see him.

I got off the phone, packed my bags up, checked out of the hotel and headed down the main street to this church that my home church used to come visit and sing at when I was younger. I just wanted to come in get a good word and some worship in. But God had other plans for me on this day. I got to the church and went in, I was there for about 20 minutes and my spirit felt funny. God was dealing with me, my spirit told me to get up and leave, as if I was in the wrong place, so I got up and I left.

Now, I realized I can watch my home church online so I tried to stream the services and they would not come up. I texted my sister Theresa and asked her if she was streaming and if church services were over. She texted me back saying they were on and she was tuned in. Well then, why can't I get them? I just felt like I was supposed to be somewhere, so I started to drive around the small town, after about 10 minutes of driving I was ready to pull over and try to stream again. So I just stopped and said a quick prayer. "Lord you know where I am supposed to be led me where you will have me to go and I will follow. In Jesus Name. Amen." Then I started to drive again, I saw a group of apartment complexes that looked like the Projects, and thought there has got to be a church back up in here. So I turned in and rode around for a few minutes, I saw a church every other corner I turned, but I did not have any desire to go in when I saw them so I spoke aloud and said "OK God, I'm going to turn down this last street and if it's not here I am going to try and stream my church again." I made that turn and then to the right I saw a Small Church

Named "Greater Love Ministries". My spirit leaped! This was it, I know just by the name this is where I am supposed to be on today. I parked my car, freshened my lip gloss, sprayed my perfume and stepped out of my car and into the church.

I was greeted at the door as I walked into the house of God. The preacher was ministering a word and my spirit felt comfortable. I was taken by the setup. It wasn't what I was used to. I walked straight in the door and to the right there were chairs that the congregation were seated in front of the pulpit, like church, but when you looked to the left there were 3 long dinner tables like someone was about to have a feast. I was puzzled. The chairs in front of the pulpit were full so I had to take a place at the table off to the side which had me thinking even more. Why are these tables here? But I shook it off for now and tuned into the service.

So the Pastor was preaching and then all of a sudden he stopped and turned his focus on some of the members. He began to talk to them. He told them that he was preaching and instead of listening to the word of God they're talking and being distractions.

Okay so now I was just thrown off, but the spirit was all over me to where I was shaking I knew I was in the right place I just had no idea why.

The pastor went on to talk to his congregation and tell them about some things that were going on financially with the church they were in need and in threat of some things being disconnected. Then he stated that he can't get the members to be faithful and pay their tithes and give offering, but in spite of it all, they feed them every Sunday after church and don't plan on stopping. Well that explained the table set up that I was wondering about. My mouth dropped in amazement just to think of if my church fed us every Sunday that would be awesome.

He went on to speak some more and told how he had been having some health issues and had to be rushed to the hospital. He also said his wife had been having some health issues and that only by God's grace they were still here. Then he turned and gave his son a few words asking what he would do with his mother and father were not around anymore, while he is acting out around their small town.

This pastor was really crying out⋯ But I still didn't know why I was there. I asked God. "Lord let this man say something and give me a word to let me know why I am here." So as the Pastor continued to speak he said the word "Parish" Ok parish, I Immediately thought John 3:16 "For God so loved the world that he gave his only begotten son, that whosoever believe in him should not parish but shall have everlasting life."

But I entered the word Parish into the Google search engine on my phone and got the passage Psalms 118:17 that reads (I shall not (parish)die, but live, and declare the works of the LORD.) My eyes bucked out of my head in amazement. I chuckled as I looked to the sky and said "God I know you're not telling me to get up and talk."

As I was in my own world with God the Pastor called for families to come together and pray. So everyone was grouped up except for yours truly. So he zeroed in on me and said "Young lady, do you have any family here?" I shook my head and replied "no sir". So he put me along with a family to pray. I walked over to the family and we began to pray. Once the pastor was finished praying I walked up to him where he stood down on the side altar and I said "excuse me sir" "Yes" he replied as he gazed at me with a different type of look, as if he knew what I was there for. "Can I say something?" I asked. He looked me square in my face and said "Yes, get in the pulpit." "Excuse me." I said, (as my mind flashed back to a word I had received from The Apostle Bill Vincent, "I see you in pulpits, and I see you bringing forth the word of God!")

The pastor then looked me right in my eyes and said very boldly "Get in the pulpit, and let God use you!" I gulped "Yes sir" I replied as I took a deep breath and climbed the 4 steps into the pulpit. I walked over and greeted the Pastors Wife and then turned stood at the podium shaking. I was literally shaking like a leaf as I prayed, God speak through me because I do not know what to say I am just a willing vessel so use me lord.

The Pastor then announces "Now we have a young lady here that has something to say to you all." Then he handed me the mic. All eyes in the building were locked on me no talking, no walking, not even a person moved they were tuned in. I went on to start speaking. "Hello everyone, my name is Keisha and I come to you from Cahokia IL/ St. Louis MO area and I can say that it is not a mistake that I stand here before you today its Gods will. If my family called me right now and said where are you? I would have to say that I don't know. I don't know the Pastor or the Co Pastors names, I don't know what street I'm on. God lead me here to speak to you all on today.

I was listening to your Pastor say that you all are not paying your tithes and offerings and your church home is going through so much. Look you must pay your tithes and give an offering because when you take care of Gods house he will turn around and bless your house and you must trust him enough to do so. I am not telling you something that I heard, I am telling you what I know. I went on to give the testimony about my church home Change Christian Church. God took the purchase price from a few million dollars down to under one million dollars. And then God graced to be paid off in a year's time. Title deed in hand! Now that was nothing but God, our praise, giving, faith and trust in him to provide and make the seemingly impossible, possible. I was blessed to be a part in that giving to my church. No matter how big or small it was to man. God blessed me with blessings in my own life just for helping to take care of his house. And God will do the same for you. There is no way that your Pastors should be going through like they are and you all are able"…. Then I turned to the Pastor and went on… "God said don't worry about anything, your church, bills, children give everything to him. You just remain faithful and God is going to bless you." Then I walked over to the Pastor and handed the microphone back to him. They clapped as I walked back to my seat. I immediately pulled out my phone and texted Theresa asking her if she can believe I just got out of these peoples pulpit because I couldn't.

The Pastor got up and thanked me for that Word, To God be the glory. Then he went on to speak to the congregation some more. They had invited me to stay for some dinner but I had to get to my visit with Mikey by 2:30 so I would not be able to.

The Co Pastors wife got up and said "We are giving toys away to a few children in the neighborhood, but word got around that we are supplying toys for all the neighborhood children, so we would like to take a love offering to help go to the store and get toys so we don't have to turn any children away." My heart was overjoyed! I was so touched to think that this church was truly living up to its name. Here they are going through struggles themselves and they still feed their congregation every Sunday and now they are blessing all the children in the neighborhood. I know a lot of places that would have said it was a mistake, only a few children would be receiving gifts. I was so happy God sent me there! I had money to shop for product to put in my store but there was no way I could not bless them with a love offering. So I planted a love offering into this ministry.

As I was heading out the Pastor greeted me and had a word for me. He told me that God was pleased with my obedience and this was just the beginning of God using me in this way. So be ready to go out different places and speak what

God says to speak. I received my word and left for my visit. I was so excited about God using me in such a big way. It was a big way to me if no one else because nothing like this had happened to me before. I thanked God for obedience and I went on my way.

Chapter 7

UNDERSTANDING

I left the church and went up to the visit I had planned with Mikey. When he sat down to the table I was so excited. He said "Hey Keisha, what's happening, how was church?" I explained to him in detail what happened and thanked him for giving me that push to go on to church on Sunday because it was not in my plans. We went on to have an amazing visit, studying the bible playing games, having snacks and fellowshipping with one another. This was a much needed weekend getaway for me, being that I was under a bit of stress back home. It felt good to get away and hang out with my best friend. I loved this guy! I was never so sure that this union was divine destiny. God had to put this together. I mean had I not come on this trip to see Mikey then I would not have been in the position to be used at Greater Love Ministries today! As I headed back home I was so joyful to God for all he was doing in my life. I was truly happy. Though I had heard that God was going to use me in a mighty way, I guess I had never really received it, until now.

About couple of weeks later I decided to pick up the phone and call the Co- Pastor Brown of the "Love Church" where I had visited while on my weekend getaway. I knew her name now because I made sure I grabbed a card with their contact information. I wanted to have a little chat with her and see how things were going with them. She answered her phone and I had to remind her who I was.

She sounded really happy to hear from me! She started to explain to me the uniqueness of their congregation. She told me that this was not your typical church with your typical Sunday crowd. They were more like an outreach ministry. They would go to the streets and get the people that may be struggling with addictions, prostitution, drinking and things of that nature. People who probably were not brought up in the church. So therefore they did not really know the importance of tithes and offerings, even though the leaders do teach them about it. Some don't have jobs and get once a month checks so therefore it only makes sense to them to pay their bills instead of give it in the offering. They really never had been taught what the scriptures say about paying tithes until they got here.

Then she went on to say that, she and her friend were just in prayer asking God to send someone to speak to their congregation in a manner that they will understand. Someone that they would listen to and pay attention and just get a clear understanding. Then on that very Sunday God sends me through their doors and put a word in my mouth for them. God is so awesome! I told her that I was grateful to God for even choosing and using me. To God be the glory and I would be back to visit with them again if the lord says the same.

Chapter 8

LOOK TO THE SKY

Not long after that weekend visit I took to see Mikey, he was once again transferred to another facility. He was moving to Columbus Corrections Center to do his last 6 months. After 2 months at this new place I went up to pay him a visit. This place was much more lenient than the last. It was an easier more smooth process getting in the door. It was a smoother visit. But when I got to the front desk they told me that they would let me in to visit Mikey this time, but he has me down on his list as a friend and would have to change that to a significant other in order for me to visit him again. That was new to me. So I told Mikey what happened in the front and after a short pause, he said he would change it. That was an eyebrow raiser to me. We had our visit, the only difference in this visit was the facility. I stayed for a few hours and left about 30 minutes early to beat the traffic.

I got in my car and headed back towards home. He was closer now so it was only a 45 minute drive. As I was riding down the highway headed home the clouds caught my eye. I looked up and there was a cloud shaped in the form of a dragon. I took a picture of it because I was so amazed, but I was trying to understand what this meant. God has spoken to me through the clouds before, but it was a hand at first···. And of course confirmation came after the hand. But now I see a dragon? This can't be good. What does this mean?

I got home and was wondering what that Dragon in the sky meant. So I started searching the Bible for scriptures and came up with Revelation 12. I was asking my friends and family members about dragons. One day Ashley came down to my house and she opened the door and screamed "I got a revelation about the dragon!" as soon as she did this the Huge black vase in my living room just fell and shattered into about 112 pieces. At that very moment I realized that on that vase···. Was a Dragon. There goes the dragon, on my beautiful vase now I had to throw it away. I was a bit sad but I figured that was my dragon because we were nowhere near the vase and it just fell and broke immediately as she came through the door saying she had an answer about the dragon. It was kind of weird and scary.

Chapter 9

LISTEN AND OBEY

Well time was winding down for Mikey, we had 3 months left until he walked up out of those gates. I almost could not believe that I had walked down 15 months by this man's side. Not without telling my family and friends and no one had a clue. Mikey and I were so close and I could talk to him about anything he really was my Spiritual Love! But yet still he was my little secret. I could hear people saying "You know how people are when they are in prison, make sure you wait and see how he will be when he gets home, because more than likely he will change." And I just did not want/need to hear that, I was already thinking about those things from time to time. But nothing would change about us being friends. Because that we were.

A few weeks later, I had an interview that I was preparing to go to, since the job; I had recently downsized leaving me unemployed. As I was getting ready, I stood in the kitchen ironing my pants, I heard a voice say "don't go" I ignored it for a minute, figuring I was just tripping and continued ironing. All of a sudden my stomach started hurting so bad to where I could not even stand, I had to go ball up on the bed. "Ok. I said I will obey. I am not going" I said. Wondering what else was in store for me, what did God want me to do, because I knew I was not going to just be without income, God has a plan and he will take care of me.

Later that week I was talking to my friend Sheena at a meeting, and letting her know that I did not know what God wanted me to do, I had been praying and asking, but still had no clarity. She asked me what can I do, and I told her that I am a writer, I can write but I don't know if that is what God wants me to do. I don't want to do anything in my own will, I don't want to choose for self anymore. I want Gods will to be done in my life. Sheena then invited me to a service at Caring Hands Ministry.

I decided to go on, I didn't have any other plans. When time came around for Prayer I went up. God spoke to me through Prophet Chandra Smith. This lady had never seen me a day in my life until this day.

She told me to lift up my hands as she anointed them, and then she said "God said pick up your pen and your pad and write." She spoke about more things to me, also about writing a book. I burst into tears, I had been writing for years, but I barely ever shared my writing with anyone. The only way people would hear what I wrote was if it was in a family member's obituary or at a funeral. I had writings stored up that I need to get out and share. At the end of the service some of the ladies were having a conversation about relationships and marriage, then Mrs. Chandra asked me if I was married. I told her not yet, but I know who my husband is and I gave them a brief description of the dream I asked for and the man that just came out of nowhere. I mean really brief, but I knew this was going to be my husband in the end. I asked them to just keep me lifted in prayer. We said our goodbyes and I left.

The next morning I awoke to a call from Mikey asking me how my job interview went a few days earlier. I explained him that I did not go to the interview because my spirit told me don't go. Now remember at this point Mikey knew me well and he knew how God had been dealing with me so I didn't expect him to act any differently other than to come into agreement with me on this situation.

Well, this time I didn't get the response I was expecting from my spiritual friend he said "maybe you should have went to the interview to make sure that's what God really said." "Really, Test God? What if Jesus decided to test God? Matthew 4:7 clearly states the scriptures also say you must not test the Lord your God! I TRUST GOD" Then he replied "aww yea that's right, God has taking care of you this for you've even been able to help me out sometimes, okay what I've got to go out call you back when I can. I love you Keisha." I said "Love you too."

Chapter 10

G-O-E

I was really disturbed in my spirit. I mean what Mikey said to me bothered me a lot, more than I ever would've thought it would. I mean why Mikey would say something like that, I don't understand. It took me long enough to start recognizing excepting and obeying when God speaks to me. And we've been in this thing together for long time now seeing signs and wonders and miracles me on the outside, as well as him on the inside.

It made me think back to when I went to hear Dr. Daniel Williams preach at a revival. He told a story about how his daughter walked away from a boyfriend because he said something about/against her father. That's exactly how I was feeling.

I know that if this person was for me or even spiritually in tune, there's no way that he would advise me to go against what I stated that God told me. That bothered me for days until I finally went to my father in prayer and asked him to reveal something to me. I asked GOD to show me of this is really the man for me, If it is not the man for me show me Lord.

I know we have developed a friendship but I was hoping for more when he got home. I need to know if we should stay friends or nothing at all. I want your will to be done God and if you say walk away then that is what I will do. Amen.

I was at the point where it was G-O-E! God over Everything! Nothing else mattered to me. I must obey God, I was out to please God. God was, is and will always be my everything! He is my first and my biggest Love!

I went to sleep and got up the next morning still bothered by me and Mikey's conversation the day before. Still thinking how could he even say that if God says something I will obey I don't care about what anyone has to say about it I already hear enough from other people close to me. Now Mikey, it saddened me.

I got up and got dressed. Me and the children were headed out to the movies when I got a text from an old friend letting me know that my ex-boyfriend, Black, was really trying to get in touch with me and wanted my phone number. Now I haven't talked to this man Black in four years but we didn't end off well so I had to think about it for minute. "Sure, you can give him my number!" I said. "Great, I will, because he is really getting on my nerves asking about you" he replied.

Not even five minutes had passed by and my phone began to ring. It was my ex-boyfriend Black on the other end of the phone. "Hey Ms. Keisha!" Black yelled in excitement. "Hey there Black, what's going on?" I replied. "I just felt I needed to call and render you an apology for the way things ended with me and you.

I never meant to hurt you Keisha, I loved you and I still do." "Well you did hurt me, but I forgave you a long time ago it's been four years, I've been let that go." I replied.

Then he went on to ask me how my children and family members and friends that he had met in our 9 months of dating were doing. He also told me that he had met my "boyfriend". Being that I was single I had no idea who he was talking about. "Boyfriend? Who?" I asked. Thinking that he ran into someone old that I use to holler at out here on the streets.

"Ole boy that's locked up at Columbus right now." He replied. "Oh. Wow! He didn't tell me he knew you." I said.

Then he said, "That's because I didn't tell him that I knew you, I didn't feel like he needed to know all of that information. I just saw a few pictures you all took when you came up to visit him, and you are looking really good by the way Miss Keisha!

But for real let me tell you this⋯ That guy isn't for you."

"Why do you say that Black?" I asked. "You're not the only person that was talking to or coming to see him. But that's all I'm telling you because I feel I owe you that much but don't ask me anything else about this situation, because I won't tell you another thing. Okay let me give you call back Keisha." I hung up the phone.

Now my mind was racing. I had no reason to trust Black at all⋯ Here is a glimpse into me and Blacks relationship. I dated Black for nine months. The night I met him we were out at 413 lounge. Black went to the rest room, I happened to be sitting next to him so I covered his drink with a napkin. When he returned he asked me if I covered his drink and when I said yes we instantly connected and we were both single so we exchanged numbers. On our first date we took a long walk on the riverfront. I thought that was so romantic, yet simple. After that we hung out often and talked daily. Spent time with each other's children, friends, family etc. all the things a couple does being that we were now considering ourselves a couple, since he had asked me to be his lady.

Well on our ninth month anniversary I graduated college and had a graduation party at the same lounge we met at. Black never showed up then my phone started ringing off the hook from a private number. The music was so loud at the party that I missed the calls, but there were voicemails on my phone. I went to the bathroom to check my voicemail and to my surprise it was a woman's voice on the other end. She said that she was Black's wife and started calling me a harlot and said I was messing with a married man. This had to happen the night of my party. I was hurt and felt betrayed I was just outdone.

Now I was an adulteress by default because Black never told me he was married/separated and allowed me to make a decision on if I wanted to go that route with him. Nope he told me he was single when all the time he was taken, a whole married man. That was the end of us and I had not to spoken to him again, until today.

So tell me why I would listen to and believe this man right now? As I rode and thought of Black giving me the info that he did, my prayer from the night before played over in my head. "God if this isn't the man for me, let me know." Then Blacks words, "He isn't the man for you".

When I made it back home I got on social media and it was like I immediately saw Ps. 55. So I opened my NLT Bible and started to read Psalms 55:11-14 which reads, "Everything is falling apart, threats and cheating are rampant in the streets. It is not an enemy who taunts me, I could bear that. It is not my foes who so arrogantly insult me, I could have hidden from them. Instead, it is you my equal, my companion and close friend. What good fellowship we once enjoyed as we walked together to the house of God. 16-17 But I will call on God and the Lord will rescue me. Morning, noon, and night I cry out in my distress and the Lord hears my voice."

The more I went before God whether I wrote him, prayed on my knees or just had a simple conversation with him like a normal person, the more he continued to speak to me through the scriptures, giving me further confirmation.

As I was sitting back talking to God, he brought back to my remembrance the dragon that I saw in the clouds the last time that I visited Mikey. I had been inquiring what that meant, and I thought that by the vase breaking that was the answer. But now that it was on my heart again I asked. "Lord please reveal to me what you were saying when you showed me that dragon in the sky. Make it so plain to me that my children can understand and explain it to someone and they would have understanding of it. In Jesus Name. Amen.

I went on with my evening. My feelings were hurting like I was on an emotional rollercoaster. I mean can I be upset about another woman? Because me and Mikey are just friends. That really wasn't a big deal to me, but not being 100%

truthful to me was. We vowed to be truthful to each other, I mean my trust was there, he had it. I remember my dad telling me when you lose a person's trust, you lose everything.

I felt cheated in a way, because I shared the truth, I told him I had male friends hung out etc. So why not be the same way and keep it real. These were the things going through my mind and I was going to let this be known. I wrote Mikey a letter asking some of these questions, as well as revealing how I had found out some things. But I did not get really detailed. I could feel this thing going downhill fast.

Chapter 11

THE TRUTH SHALL SET YOU FREE

A few days later as I was getting ready to head out to revival, my phone rang. Ring, ring. "Hello" I said. Then I hear Mikey's voice "Hey Keish! What's up Love? I've been missing you! So let me know what's up with this letter you sent me, I thought we were better than this here, how can you just let someone talk about me in this way and you just listen to them and believe anything. Who told you these things? Who's slandering my name like this?"

My blood was boiling from all of the built up emotions waiting on this phone call. I blew up on Mikey, "Look Mikey, your game is up. I don't know why you're asking what the letter means, you can read and comprehend, it means just what it said, and you have no problem understanding!"

Then he said "Wow Keisha, if you believe what another dude is telling you about me, then what's that saying about you? If that's the kind of friend you are, we don't need to be friends!" "Ok." I replied as I hung up the phone.

I sat back and thought on some of the things he had expressed, wondering if it was just me tripping just listening to someone else. I mean I had been conversing and spending time with this man for 15 months now···. I love him.

So many thoughts were going through my mind. (An Idle mind is the devils playground) The devil is a liar! I jumped up grabbed my keys and headed to the revival meeting at Revival Waves of Glory. The Apostle Bill Vincent always delivered a good word, and I needed a word right now. I made it to the revival and listened to the teaching and gave God the praise! At the end of the service, I went out in the lobby to purchase a cd. As I was out there I saw a clearance basket.

As I looked through the basket I pulled up a cd with a picture on the front of the case. My mouth dropped at what I saw.

The cd was titled "Spiritual Warfare" and there was a split picture that had Jesus on a white horse on one side on the other side there was a dragon breathing fire, and in front of the fire was the word "LIES". I was blown away. Now I know when I talk to God and ask him, he answers me, and it doesn't take long. I mean I'm literally getting responses to the things I ask on the next day, or at least within the week.

From that point on it was me and God. I stayed in his face, I longed to hear from him. The Bible says in Matthew 6:33 Seek the Kingdom of God above all else, and live righteously, and he will give you everything you need. So it was me and God. I chased after God profusely.

A month had gone by, I had gotten calls from Mikey but I wouldn't even answer them. I was missing him and our conversations though, but I had to accept that he was not "the one". So if anything we would be friends only and nothing else was going to become of us. But that is not always easy for people to accept. Sometimes your feelings can go deeper than wanting to remain friends. I mean it's like with any relationship you spend your time in, you become attached.

As I sat at my kitchen table finishing up my writing on a spoken word piece I was doing for an event coming up, I stopped and asked God a question. "God, can I talk to Mikey?" I then looked to my right and a bible was there. It was The Good News Bible TodaYs English VerSion. That YES in Todays English Version jumped out at me. So I started to write Mikey a letter, letting him know how I was feeling. I knew I did not let him say much when I spoke to him and it was mainly because I didn't want to hear more lies. I told him things that were on my heart and in my spirit, sent a couple of scriptures and sealed the envelope that I placed the letter in. I then drifted right off to sleep.

The next morning I woke up to my phone ringing, I rolled over and looked at the phone and it was Mikey. Ok now this was mind blowing to me The Bible says in Matthew 7:7 "Keep on asking, and you will receive what you ask for. Keep on seeking, and you will find. Keep on knocking, and the door will be opened to you." And when I ask for things God was answering and giving them to me. I was getting confirmations and manifestation these things were happening right before my very eyes. If I didn't have crazy faith or trust before now⋯. I had it now. These things that were happening were not coincidences, it was GOD!

I answered the phone and he just started conversing as if nothing ever happened. He let me know that he appreciated me and my friendship very much and wouldn't want to hurt me. Blah blah blah is all I was hearing. It was really not anything I wanted to hear, but there was something that I needed to see. I said "you have one last visit this weekend before you come home and I'm going to come visit." He agreed I should come.

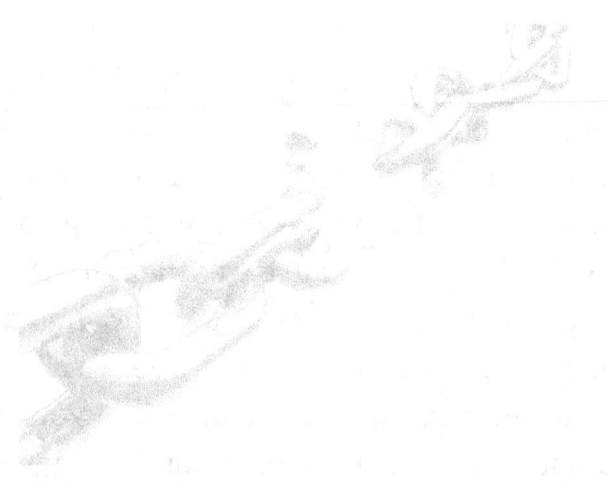

Chapter 12

RELEASED

The weekend was here before I knew it. I got up praying to God and getting myself ready then went on up to Distant Correctional Center. Now I went in with an expectancy that things would be different than the other visits this I already knew. I was also ready for the questions about who issued me the information I had found out about him. When I entered the facility I was assigned the table as usual. I went and sat down and waited on Mikey's arrival. Mikey came out to the visiting room and the feeling was totally different. I had the Bible on the table and the playing cards. Mikey came up out of the gate asking questions and acting out of order. He was saying things that he never said to me before, profound disrespectful things. His hands were trying to wander all over parts of my body where they shouldn't have. I was constantly smacking his hands, then I expressed to him that I would break his finger if he attempted to touch me again. Mikey's true colors were starting to shine through. This is not the same person I had been talking to the last 17 months. But I had to see this to further let me know this was not the man for me, it was confirming the fire breathing dragon. LIES! All I could do is look at Mikey and shake my head in disbelief.

I couldn't believe it then I started feeling like this visit was about to come to an end. At that moment a female guard walked up and said "Mr. Mason come with me the Chief wants to see you." I knew for sure the visit was over then. I instantly began to pray Gods covering over Mikey. Because I knew these people watch every move that we make in these visiting rooms and he was truly out of order with his actions. I nearly had to fight him off.

As I sat alone for about 10 minutes the female guard came up to me and said your visit is now over I will walk you up to the front and explain. As we walked through the steel doors she explained that his visit had been terminated due to Mikey's inappropriate behavior. She said that they had been watching and saw him continually trying to touch me inappropriately and saw me fighting him off. They just decided to terminate the rest of his visit instead of taking further measures being that he only had a week left. I knew that was a blessing from God because they will issue more time for the smallest of things in those facilities.

Mikey must have called me at least 10 times on my ride home, but I just pressed ignore and sat back and talked to God and thanked him for revelation. I really did not want to speak to Mikey I was very disappointed in him. I felt like this was my release from him. I mean to be kicked out of a visiting room was crazy. But I already knew this was going to be different than any other time. And indeed it was.

About 3 days had passed and Mikey reached out again. I answered the phone this time. He said that he had been calling me to make sure I was ok and see what the lady said to me when she let me out of the visiting room. Before I could say anything he went on to say that they said he was behaving inappropriately and they saw him on camera, he said they were tripping he did nothing of the sort. I couldn't believe what I was hearing. I "So you were not acting inappropriately Mikey? You were not trying to get your feel on?" "No! I wasn't" He replied. This dude was obviously crazy, or just a liar. But I knew that much by now. I should've know his nickname was "Sly" for a reason.

He had been telling me that he was going to take the bus home but I didn't believe that for one second. I knew he was eventually going to either ask me for a ride from the station or a ride home. And low and behold he asked me if I could come and get him. My spirit and everything else within me said No, but I was trying to be nice because I figured that he really didn't have anyone else that was dealing with him like I had been all this time. Plus I cared about him. I mean I had been there through thick and thin. Praying, fasting, studying, and just being a true friend, so I told him I would come.

2 days later Mikey walked out of those prison doors and packed his belongings in the back of my SUV. He kept saying, "I'm Free I'm Free, it feels so funny. I ain't never looking back, Prison will not see me again." I immediately pulled over on the McDonalds lot and whipped out my blessed

oil and anointed him and we prayed together. I got on the highway and headed down 55 to his mother's house. The whole ride home I just kept hearing, "Man Keisha I owe you big-time, you stuck by my side, looked out for me nobody else did, for a whole year and a half. Anything I get I will make sure I help you out in every way possible. Because you truly have been there for me when you didn't have to. And I Love and appreciate you! I promise I am about to show you that now." When we got to his mom's house I let him out the car he said he would call me later then we both went our separate ways.

So now in my mind, we should at least be able to remain friends. I mean it couldn't hurt to remain friends and maybe hang out from time to time right. I have spent this much time with him behind bars now he is free so we should hang out. I didn't want to think about me being released from him before he came home. Maybe it will be ok now that he is home free, at least sometimes.

Mikey and I stayed in touch and hung out a few times. One Sunday he attended church with me, and on that day God showed up and out in the service. God even used me in such a mighty way that Mikey could witness to, but at the same time reveling gifting's and abilities to me that he has blessed me with. I take my relationship with God and the life I live for him seriously. I don't play when it comes to God because he has been so good to me.

But some people are not use to people Walking Gods way for real, in line with God's word. I was truly striving to please God.

Chapter 13

LETTING GO

Mikey and I hung out every single week at least once a week, but things weren't that great between us. We would argue a lot and we were only friends. God would give me a word, or I would say something to him and he just would instantly start to go against what I said and start an argument. He did not like for me to speak what God said to him at all. I guess it was just me. I don't know. But I open my mouth and speak if God tells me to.

I remember when Mikey came to my house for the first time and looked at my pictures on my wall and said that I had a beautiful family as far as my siblings and in-laws. He would always compliment everyone and everything except for me. One day, I got my hair done and saw him that same day, he said to me "You think you are all that because you got your hair done." I was really just expecting a compliment, being that he was the compliment King when it came to others. I remember thinking "What is his problem when it comes to me?", I didn't understand at all.

Some things he would say would have broken me down if I was a weak enough female or had low self-esteem. Because some things he would say were unnecessary and to me they were put downs. Sometimes I felt like he was trying to break my spirit. He would say sly things and then remind me that we are only friends, like people do when you don't want to get in a relationship. But neither one of us were pressing to be in a relationship at the moment. So he was really throwing me off.

While at my house, we started looking through some pictures. Mikey saw a picture of one of my family members and told me that she was blessed. "You don't know her so, what you mean?" I asked. He said "you know what I mean… She is blessed with that thing on her back."

My facial expression instantly turned. "That was just disrespectful", I implied and he then said. "It's the truth, most men look and won't tell you, I'm just keeping it real. We are just friends right Keisha? You shouldn't care about that." I still felt there was a line that you just don't cross, and he had crossed that line a few times now.

I was over Mikey at that point, because the more he reminded me of our "friendship" the more I thought back to all the letters he wrote, talking about making me his wife, and being together. So if I did reveal my secret to people while Mikey was still in jail, and listen to them say I should be careful because he will probably change once he gets out. Then they would have been telling me the truth about this one. Plus I knew I did not want to be in a relationship with this man anyway, not now after all this mess. The furthest we could ever go is friendship.

One day Mikey and I were talking and he told me that he wanted to be a provider and a protector, just as the Bible says. He wanted a wife, kids, dog, just to live a normal life. I said "really, Ok. That sounds wonderful!"

I went to sleep that night and had a dream. The dream went throughout several locations, but the last location was on the altar of the church. It was Mikey's wedding. Mikey was handsomely dressed in all white as was his bride with her vale. It looked like it was a beautiful wedding, with two happy people who were probably made for one another.

I woke up the next morning and reached out to Mikey. I said "hey Mikey, I had a dream about you last night, I saw your wedding and your wife, but I wasn't in the picture anywhere, I am not your wife. "

As I told him this he got furious and started to argue with me asking me how do I know? And maybe God is working on us to be together. I thought it was nuts. This man clearly has the way of showing a woman genuine Love and interest mixed up. I guess he was still in the 3rd grade mentality because the way he acted, put me down, reminded me we were only friends often, and disrespect that he thought was just "keeping it real" was crazy to me. And to think that I would have a second thought on being with someone who is gawking at my family members hind parts and expressing it to me is outlandish. That's not how I get down.

The next time Mikey called me, I went to pick him up after he had worked an odd end job, he got in the car with me and suggested that we ate a meal together and watched movies, I was cool with that. He asked me to order from this little place I go to called the "Chicken Spot" so I called and placed our order. When we got there he asked me to come inside with him, so I did.

The clerk told him the price "$10.75 please" He then looked at me and said "Keisha, how can I pay for this when I have no money?" My mouth dropped. I was so mad I could have blown up on him right in that place. But I didn't. I pulled out my last $20 and paid for the meal. No one knew it was my last $20 but me and God. I went back and sat in the car as Mikey went into the store next door. He asked me if I wanted anything and I said a pack of gum. I was so mad sitting in that car I could have cried. But I shook it off and said to myself, this is it Keisha. No more, it's time.

Mikey got in the car and we headed to my house to watch movies. As I laid on the couch and looked at the TV Mikey sat behind me in the Wicker chair. It was such an amazing thing that just took place in the movie I quickly turned to Mikey to say something to catch him sipping on a bottle of Hennessey, but he tried to tuck it away quickly. I asked "What was that?" "Nothing he said, Keisha you just tripping girl, what were you asking me about the movie?"

I just turned around and continued watching the movie. Now my blood was boiling, I was upset and hurt. Just to think that the things I did for Mikey in all this time I did out of love so it was nothing that I would just throw up in his face. But at this moment all I could think was that this man would not even sacrifice to buy me a funky plate of chicken, after all that I have done for him. If I had never been through before I was so through now. This was it! After the movie I took Mikey home. His words to me as he got out of the car were "It's not strange, I know you don't love me!" then he closed the door. I looked at this guy like he was nuts and shook my head in disbelief. I had shown this man nothing but pure unadulterated love. I was not overlooking another thing that he did at this point. I made it back home and went through my cell phone and blocked every number that Mikey would call from, I blocked the text messages also. I meant I was done.

The lying, back and forth bickering, arguing then friends again was getting on my nerves. He had only been home for 2 months now and I cared for him. But what kind of friendship was this? Notice that I said I, not God. I was doing what I felt right God didn't tell me to keep going around this man as a matter of fact I was released from him, before I went to pick him up on his out date. After that last visit up to Columbus Correctional Center, it was all me. God had already told me, shown me, and released me from this circumstance. This all was my doing, holding on to something, because of my feelings, that I should've been let go of a while ago.

That night when I went to sleep I had a dream. Now I normally don't remember the dreams that I have so when I do I know they mean something. I was sitting in a booth at a restaurant with my girl-friend and her man. We were on a double date and I was so close to the guy next to me. I was just laying all over his chest like I was so comfortable with this man, but it was our first date. This man was my husband, and I knew it. And he was everything that I ever wanted as far as appearance so I didn't have to settle not one bit. I woke up and God told me this was the dream I had prayed for almost 2 years ago. I was so happy that I had finally had my dream that I prayed for. Me, Keisha no one else had it, it was me. Now I know he isn't that far away. But I had to finally walk away from what was holding me back from moving forward towards my destiny. That's Deep!

We all know that there is a Reason for some, a Season for some people in our lives and others are meant to be around for a lifetime. When a person's reason or season is up, and God says walk away or gives you an exit of escape, then we need to yield to it. God provides us with Stop signs along with Exit ramps. When the ride is over and it is time to hop off then we need to do just that. Just because you are walking away does not mean that you did not Love or are not showing love. You can still Love a person, after all God is Love and though we don't see him with the naked eye he is always there!

God never leaves us blind, but when we decide to try and follow our own will instead of God's will for us then we place our own selves in a bind that sometimes people have a hard time getting out of. Then we cry out to God when we could have just walked in obedience when God tried to get us out of the situation in the first place. Just Trust and Obey God!

A few days later as I was riding down the street I heard Gods voice so clearly, He said "Prison Break" at that very moment I understood. That was the whole purpose of this Union. The purpose of me going through what I did with this man was to break me in, Increase my faith, my trust in God and move to higher levels. It was the key to unlock and show me how to walk in some of the giftings that God has placed on my life. I had to get out of my "Comfort Zone" and receive this story/testimony to share with and uplift others. This is my story, I did not write this book to bash men that are in prison, or say they are all bad people. I am just telling my story the way that it went. And it included a man that was behind bars.

Being broken is not fun and some breaks are more painful than others. Some women have been in this same situation and have been broken in a whole different kind of way. Some get with prisoners or even become imprisoned by men that just break them down. Some women are with men that are not even in prison but just break them down emotionally, and physically with control mechanisms. Some women lose their identity during the process. Some people will try to take advantage of you if you let them. But it is all up to us how much we decided to accept from another person. We all will go through a break in our lives, but I say that it is time to break the chains of Bondage! Be Free!

When you are broken in any way then God can fix you. God showed me that the reason for this relationship was for God to get all the glory. God showed me 3 months before this man came home that he was not the one. Did I walk away and stay away immediately? No. I went on and made my own choices to stick around and try to remain friends because I felt like 18 months of my life was a long time to spend waiting on someone. Also, I cared about him, so I did not want to walk away, he had a piece of my heart.

I have not had a conversation with Mikey since that day. We have sent a few texts and he is not happy with me for walking away. It was hard because Mikey was a part of my growth and preparation process, and I thank God for him and wish him the best. But if I decided to stay around longer just because I wanted to, things could have gotten out of control. I could have lost my identity along the way. I didn't chose this path I was Chosen for it! I prayed a simple prayer and this all came from that one prayer. Now I am sharing a whole book with you all.

I've learned over time that we have to stop choosing people and things on our own, and then thinking that things will work out because they won't work out like they would if it's blessed by God.

When God tells us to let go of things and walk away, it's not always easy especially when it is a person or a thing that we are familiar with and do not want to let go. We just want to stick around and pray that things will change and make things work. Well, nothing will work like it is supposed to if God is not at the core of it. Because what God ordains he will maintain, and when God is in it, there are No Limits on where it can go!

I thank God for my struggles, for my trials, I thank God for this year and a half run that I've had. Because it has gotten me ready for the rest of my life with the man that I am supposed to be with. A man with eyes for me, a heart for me, and that man will truly be my best friend, my protector and provider, my head. He will uplift and encourage me at all times in whatever I do, He will not say a thing that can potentially break me down and he will be happy with me… Keisha, my imperfections, flaws and all. He will love me for me and he will be a man after Gods own heart. There will be no more imitations, when he comes he will be "The Real Thing" Ha! Ain't nothing like the real thing baby!

Now I am at a place where I feel like I am ready, I am ready for my next level as far as a relationship goes. I have been in preparation as far as this walk I just took. I believe I was taken through this so that I could learn how to pray for my mate, to declare and decree things over my mate, speak up for my mate, Believe things for/with my mate, walk in the spirit more, also to elevate my faith.

I have seen God move more now through this process as I prayed, fasted, and believed the things that I prayed and spoke over this man as well as myself would come to pass. Also the things that I asked God and he answered me and showed me everything I asked him. I stayed in the spirit to the point where I was going out where God sent me and speaking what he told me to say. That's real spiritual growth for me.

God will do just what he said, it doesn't matter what it looks like, God will fulfill his promises that he made. And God promised me some things and I am just waiting on those things to manifest because he promised it, I believe it is already done. And that is not just for me, he can and will do the same thing for you!

So I scream To God be the glory for this break-through! Keep God first in all that you do. There is no one greater than God and that is who we should all live and strive to please. God first, Not a man, a woman, not a child, nor anybody else, as long as God is pleased with you then everything else will fall into place and he will never lead you wrong. And if you follow him everything will be all right!

B Blessed

I would like to extend special thanks everyone at Revival Waves of Glory Publishing for their assistance in every way that it was rendered. May God continue to bless them abundantly!

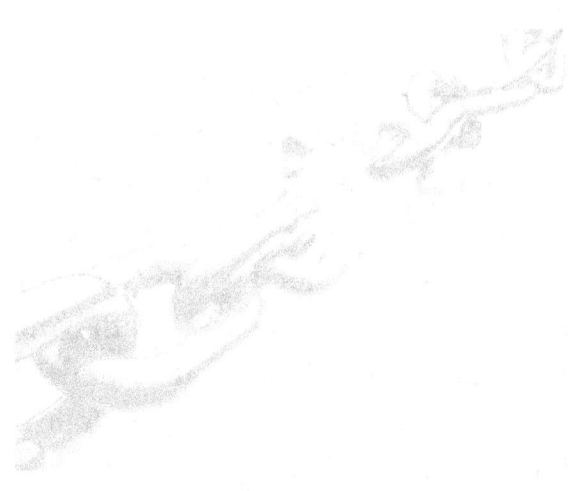

www.ingramcontent.com/pod-product-compliance
Lightning Source LLC
Chambersburg PA
CBHW072102290426
44110CB00014B/1786